W9-DBJ-776

RACE FOR YOUR LIFE!

THE INDIANAPOLIS 500

BY KATE MIKOLEY

HOT TOPICS

Please visit our website, www.garethstevens.com. For a free color catalog of all our high-quality books, call toll free 1-800-542-2595 or fax 1-877-542-2596.

Cataloging-in-Publication Data

Names: Mikoley, Kate.
Title: The Indianapolis 500 / Kate Mikoley.
Description: New York : Gareth Stevens Publishing, 2021. | Series: Race for your life! | Includes glossary and index.
Identifiers: ISBN 9781538259061 (pbk.) | ISBN 9781538259085 (library bound) | ISBN 9781538259078 (6 pack)
Subjects: LCSH: Indianapolis Speedway Race–Juvenile literature. | Automobile racing--United States–Juvenile literature.
Classification: LCC GV1033.5.I55 M57 2021 | DDC 796.7206'877252–dc23

First Edition

Published in 2021 by
Gareth Stevens Publishing
111 East 14th Street, Suite 349
New York, NY 10003

Designer: Laura Bowen
Editor: Kate Mikoley

Photo credits: Cover, pp. 1–32 (texture) Chatham172/Shutterstock.com; Cover, pp. 1 (car), 5, 17, 19 (bottom), 23, 25 Icon Sportswire/Contributor/Icon Sportswire/Getty Images; pp. 7, 11 Bettmann/Contributor/Bettmann/Getty Images; p. 9 ANN MILLER CARR/Contributor/AFP/Getty Images; p. 13 Chris Graythen/Staff/Getty Images Sport/Getty Images; p. 15 KEREM YUCEL/Contributor/AFP/Getty Images; p. 19 (top) Todd Warshaw/Stringer/Getty Images Sports/Getty Images; p. 21 Patrick Smith/Staff/Getty Images Sports/Getty Images; p. 27 Clive Rose/Staff/Getty Images Sport/Getty Images; p. 29 Robert Laberge/Stringer/Getty Images Sport/Getty Images.

Printed in the United States of America

CPSIA compliance information: Batch #CS20GS: For further information contact Gareth Stevens, New York, New York at 1-800-542-2595.

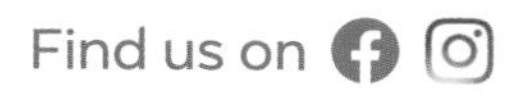

CONTENTS

THE GREATEST SPECTACLE IN RACING

Indianapolis is the capital of Indiana, but the city is also known for being home to "The Greatest **Spectacle** in Racing"—the Indianapolis 500. Simply called the Indy 500, this car race draws huge crowds. It's held each year over Memorial Day weekend.

FEARLESS FACTS

The Indy 500 really takes place in a town within the city of Indianapolis, called Speedway, Indiana.

INDY HISTORY

Except for a few years during World War I and World War II, the Indy 500 has been held every year since 1911. The 500-mile (805 km) race takes place at the Indianapolis **Motor** Speedway. The speedway, or track, was built in 1909 to test cars.

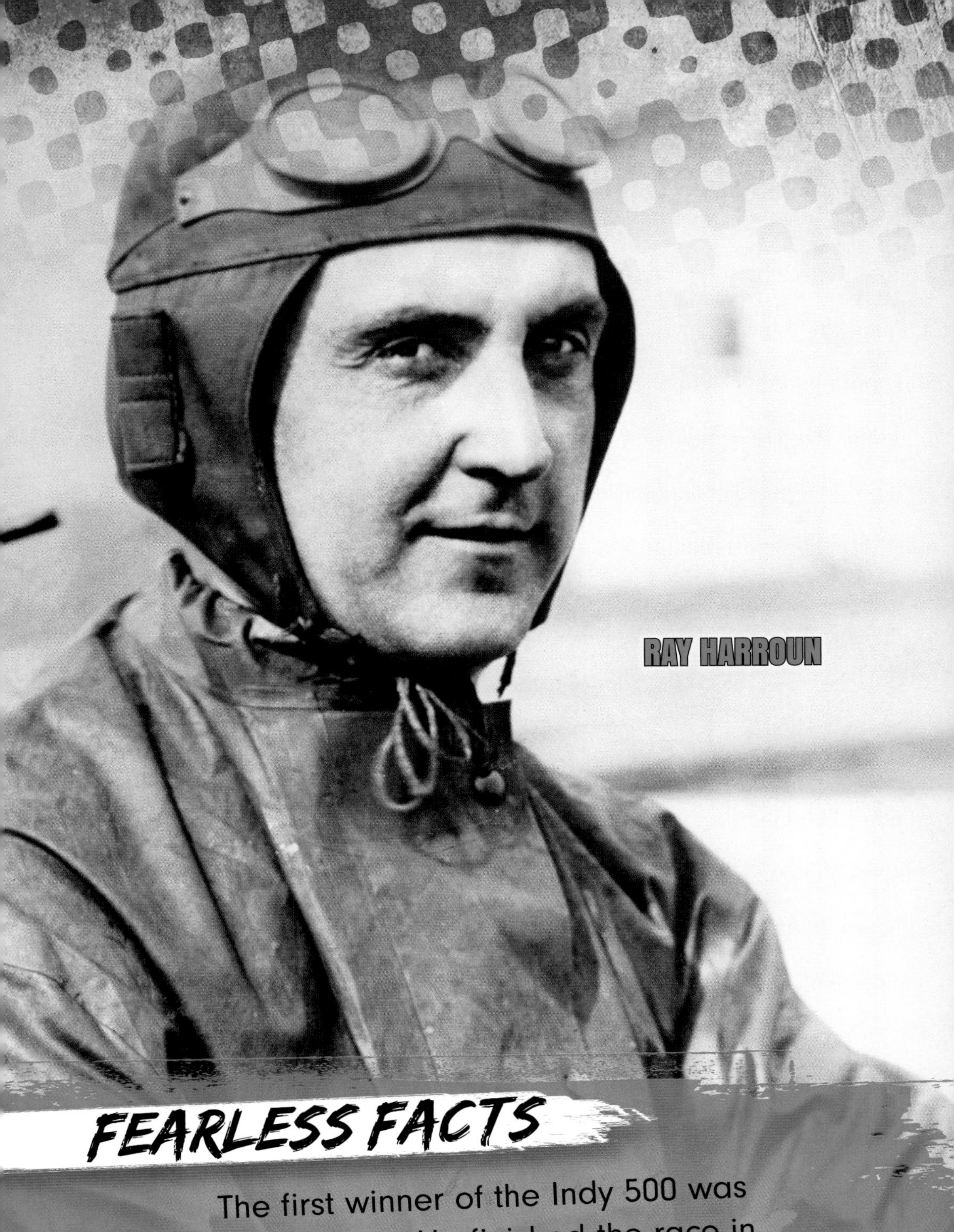
RAY HARROUN

FEARLESS FACTS

The first winner of the Indy 500 was Ray Harroun. He finished the race in 6 hours, 42 minutes, and 8 seconds.

THE BRICKYARD

The Indianapolis Motor Speedway is often called the Brickyard. Soon after it was built, the track was covered in **brick**. It has since been covered in asphalt, a material used to make roads. Still, the nickname stuck.

FEARLESS FACTS

Today, 36 inches (91.4 cm) of the original brick remains at the starting and finish line of the track. Winners at the speedway often celebrate by kissing the bricks.

The track at the Indianapolis Motor Speedway is 2.5 miles (4 km) around. It's shaped like a rectangle with rounded corners. This is called a rectangular oval. In the Indy 500, drivers take 200 laps of the track.

FEARLESS FACTS

Drivers in the Indy 500 sometimes reach speeds faster than 220 miles (354 km) per hour!

THE CARS

The cars used in the Indy 500 are fittingly called IndyCars. Unlike the cars you may see in other kinds of races, IndyCars have open wheels and are close to the ground. The driver sits in an open cockpit.

FEARLESS FACTS

Today, the Indianapolis 500 is part of a series, or group, of races called the IndyCar Series. It's the most famous event in the series.

WATCHING THE RACE

The Indy 500 draws hundreds of thousands of fans to the Indianapolis Motor Speedway each year. It's one of the most highly attended one-day sporting events in the world. Even more people watch the race on TV.

FEARLESS FACTS

The Indianapolis Motor Speedway has seats for more than 250,000 people, but more can be added. In some years, more than 400,000 fans attended the Indy 500!

ON THE TRACK

Over the years, the number of cars allowed in the Indy 500 has changed. The race has seen as few as 21 and as many as 42 cars battle it out for the win. Today, 33 cars take part in the event.

FEARLESS FACTS

It was decided that keeping the event at 33 cars would allow for a good amount of room between each car. However, cars can still get very close and crashes do happen!

GETTING TO THE STARTING LINE

Before someone can be in the Indy 500, they have to **qualify**. Qualifying runs take place days before the race. Drivers take runs of four laps of the track. The fastest drivers get a spot in the race.

FEARLESS FACTS

During qualifying runs, drivers go one at a time. This keeps the track clear so drivers can go as fast as possible.

The 33 cars that make it to race day start off in rows of three. A car's position at the start depends on how fast it went during the qualifying runs. The fastest car during qualifying runs gets to start at a spot called the pole position.

FEARLESS FACTS

The pole position is the inside spot in the first row. It's considered the best place to start.

RACING AHEAD

The driver in pole position doesn't have to get past any other cars to be in the lead at the start. However, this doesn't mean they'll win. Drivers who have started in pole position have won the Indy 500 about 20 percent of the time.

FEARLESS FACTS

Drivers who start in the middle or back of the pack often pull ahead. People have won the race with starting positions as high as 28!

Some drivers use drafting to get ahead. This is a method of driving closely behind another car. It lessens wind **resistance** and helps drivers gain speed more easily. When they get a chance, they can then move over and make their way to the front.

FEARLESS FACTS

Pit stops allow for tire changes and quick repairs, or fixes, during the race. Crews can change all four tires, add **fuel**, and make other repairs in less than 10 seconds.

THE TROPHY

The winner of the Indianapolis 500 gets the Borg-Warner **Trophy**. First given out in 1936, the trophy includes the faces of every person who has won the race! Over the years, parts have been added to the trophy to fit more faces.

FEARLESS FACTS

Winners also get prize money. In 2019, the top prize was more than $2.6 million! The other drivers win money too. Even a last-place finisher can make around $200,000.

DRINKING THE MILK

In 1936, Louis Meyer drank buttermilk after winning the race. Someone in the milk business thought this could help sell milk. Except for the years 1947 to 1955, every winner since 1936 has celebrated their win by drinking milk!

FEARLESS FACTS

Buttermilk is the leftover liquid from when milk or cream is used to make butter. Winners of the Indy 500 now drink regular cow's milk after the race.

RACING SAFETY TIPS

KNOW AND FOLLOW ALL RULES OF THE RACE

WEAR SAFETY GEAR, INCLUDING A HELMET AND SPECIAL CLOTHING THAT DOESN'T EASILY CATCH FIRE

WEAR A SEATBELT

MAKE SURE THE CAR MEETS RACE RULES AND PASSES ALL TESTS

WATCH FOR WARNINGS, OFTEN GIVEN BY FLAGS AND LIGHTS, ABOUT TROUBLE ON THE TRACK

FOR MORE INFORMATION

BOOKS

Braulick, Carrie A. *Indy Cars.* North Mankato, MN: Capstone Press, 2019.

Fishman, Jon M. *Cool Indy Cars.* Minneapolis, MN: Lerner Publications, 2019.

Wolkin, Joseph Steven. *Superfast Indy Car Racing.* Minneapolis, MN: Lerner Publications, 2020.

WEBSITES

10 Things You May Not Know About the Indianapolis 500
www.history.com/news/10-things-you-may-not-know-about-the-indianapolis-500
Find out more about this famous event here.

Indy 500
www.indianapolismotorspeedway.com/events/indy500
Discover more about the Indianapolis 500.

What Is Pole Position?
www.wonderopolis.org/wonder/what-is-pole-position
Learn more about pole position and how it's decided at the Indy 500.

Publisher's note to educators and parents: Our editors have carefully reviewed these websites to ensure that they are suitable for students. Many websites change frequently, however, and we cannot guarantee that a site's future contents will continue to meet our high standards of quality and educational value. Be advised that students should be closely supervised whenever they access the internet.

GLOSSARY

brick: a small, hard block of baked clay used for building

fuel: something used to make energy, heat, or power

motor: a machine that produces motion or power for doing work

qualify: to show the necessary skills or knowledge to do a certain activity

resistance: a force that slows a moving object by going against the direction the object is moving

spectacle: something that gets attention because it is very unusual or notable

trophy: a prize given to the winner of a race